CHILDREN OF ST. MARTHA
SCHOOL LIBRARY

No Level

14.36

HOW OUR BODIES WORK
The FIVE SENSES
JACQUELINE DINEEN

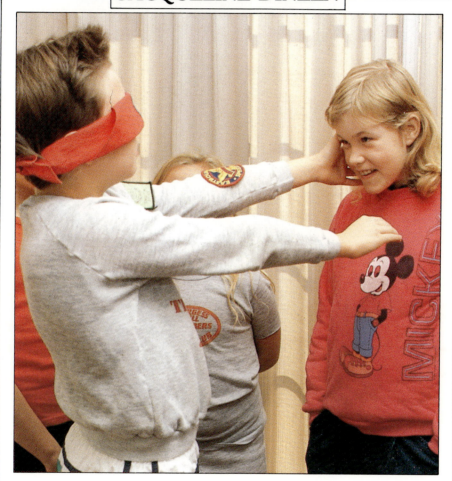

Editorial planning
Philip Steele

MACMILLAN

© Macmillan Education Limited 1989
© BLA Publishing Limited 1989

All rights reserved. No reproduction, copy or transmission of this publication may be made without written permission.

No paragraph of this publication may be reproduced, copied or transmitted save with written permission or in accordance with the provisions of the Copyright Act 1956 (as amended), or under the terms of any licence permitted limited copying issued by the Copyright Licensing Agency, 33–4 Alfred Place, London, WC1E 7DP.

Any person who does any unauthorised act in relation to this publication may be liable to criminal prosecution and civil claims for damages.

First published 1989

Published by
MACMILLAN EDUCATION LTD
Houndmills, Basingstoke, Hampshire RG21 2XS
and London
Companies and representatives
throughout the world

Designed and produced by BLA Publishing Limited,
East Grinstead, Sussex, England.

Also in LONDON · HONG KONG · TAIPEI · SINGAPORE · NEW YORK

A Ling Kee Company

Illustrations by Val Sangster/Linden Artists and Linda Thursby/Linden Artists
Colour origination by Chris Waterden Reproductions
Printed in Hong Kong

British Library Cataloguing in Publication Data

Dineen, Jacqueline
　The five senses. — (How our bodies work)
　— (Macmillan world library)
　1. Senses and sensation — Juvenile literature
　I. Title　II. Steele, Philip　III. Series
　612'.8　QP434

ISBN 0-333-45966-0

Photographic credits

t = top b = bottom l = left r = right

cover: Trevor Hill

4t Sporting Pictures; 4b Science Photo Library; 5 Mountain Camera; 6 The Hutchison Library; 7t Vivien Fifield; 7b Mary Evans Picture Library; 8 Science Photo Library; 9 Rex Features; 11, 13t, 13b, 14 Trevor Hill; 15t J. Allan Cash; 15b Trevor Hill; 16 Science Photo Library; 17, 19t, 19b, 21t, 21b Trevor Hill; 23t, 23b J. Allan Cash; 24 ZEFA; 25, 26 Trevor Hill; 27t, 27b Science Photo Library; 29t, 29b, 31t, 31b, 32 Trevor Hill; 33t J. Allan Cash; 33, 34t, 34b, 35 Trevor Hill; 36 The Guide Dogs for the Blind Association; 37t, 37b Science Photo Library; 38 Trevor Hill; 39t Twinings; 39b J. Allan Cash; 40 ZEFA; 41t Chris Fairclough Picture Library; 41b Mountain Camera; 43 Trevor Hill; 44 Frank Lane Picture Library; 45t, 45b Science Photo Library

---

Note to the reader
In this book there are some words in the text which are printed in **bold** type. This shows that the word is listed in the glossary on page 46. The glossary gives a brief explanation of words which may be new to you.

Contents

Introduction	4	How the eye works	28
Finding out	6	Eye tests	30
A network of nerves	8	Problems with the eyes	32
Senses and the brain	10	Treating eyes	34
Skin and touch	12	Blindness	36
Using touch	14	Lost to the world	38
Tasting food	16	Safety first	40
A sense of smell	18	To the rescue	42
How we hear	20	Did you know?	44
Ears and balance	22		
Hearing problems	24	Glossary	46
Coping with deafness	26	Index	48

Introduction

Your **senses** tell you what is going on in the world around you. What are senses? You are using one of your senses to read this book. Your eyes see the words on the page and the colours in the pictures. Your eyes give you your sense of sight. The other senses are touch, taste, smell, and hearing. Without these senses you could not recognize anything. You could not enjoy the world around you. You would not know when to run away from danger.

Suppose you meet a friend in the street. Your eyes see the person and send a message to your **brain**. Messages are passed to and from the brain along a network of **nerves**. Your brain controls everything you do. Your brain recognizes your friend. You stop and say hello. Your friend speaks and your ears send another message to your brain. The brain sorts out all the information from the senses.

▲ Boris Becker, the West German tennis player is concentrating hard. All his senses are working as he waits for his opponent to serve the ball. Most of us use our senses every day without even thinking about them.

◀ The human eye has one lens. The round eyes of a dragonfly have up to 30 000 lenses. The dragonfly relies only on its sense of sight to catch insects for food.

Introduction

▶ A dog's sense of smell is about 100 times better than a human being's. By sniffing, this German Shepherd dog can find someone buried deep under the snow. The dog is trained to recognize the scent of a human being.

Animal senses

Human beings are part of the animal world. All animals have senses. Most humans use all five senses to tell them about the world around them. Other animals do not have all these senses. They have strong senses which suit their own lives. Most birds cannot smell much. They have very good sight instead. They use their eyes to find food, such as brightly coloured berries and fruit. A peregrine falcon hunts other animals for food. This bird can see a pigeon as far away as eight kilometres. The kiwi of New Zealand does have a good sense of smell and touch. It has a long beak with bristles around it. The bird burrows into earth and leaves with its beak. It can smell insects and feel them.

Animals which hunt at night, such as cats and owls, have eyes which can see very well in the dark. Some fish have huge eyes which can see in the darkness of the deep oceans.

Insects have a good sense of smell. A male emperor moth can smell a female emperor moth 11 kilometres away. Bees can smell the sweet scent of flowers from a long way away. The long feelers on an insect's head are for feeling and smelling.

Staying alive

All animals need their senses to stay alive. Without them, they could not feel pain or escape from their enemies. This book is about human senses and how we use them.

Finding out

Thousands of years ago, people had to hunt for their food. Their senses had to be very sharp. They used their eyes to see animals hiding in the forests and to follow their tracks. They could smell the animals with their noses, and their sharp ears picked up the sounds of cracking twigs. Today most people do not have to hunt. They take their senses for granted. They use their senses for pleasures, like listening to music.

The early hunters did not understand how their senses worked. It took thousands of years for people to find out about them. Then doctors began to study the senses. Scientists invented instruments to help people with bad sight and hearing.

Long ago

The study of medicine began in ancient Greece. The Greek doctor Hippocrates is known as the 'father of medicine'. He was born on the island of Cos over 2000 years ago. Hippocrates was the first person to link the brain with the senses, though no one knew how the senses worked. Blindness was common. Eye doctors travelled through the Roman Empire treating blind people with soothing medicines. There were no **spectacles** until about 700 years ago. The first spectacles were made in Venice. They were also worn in China at that time. There was very little help for deaf people until about 300 years ago, when the first ear trumpets were made.

▼ In some parts of the world, people still hunt for food just as our ancestors did. They need very sharp senses. They watch for animals and listen hard for sounds of movement in the trees. The hunter must also look out for animals hunting him!

Finding out

▲ An eye doctor treats a patient, about 400 years ago. There were new treatments for blindness at this time. Doctors were only just beginning to understand how our senses work.

The age of science

An Italian scientist was the first person to find out how our bodies move. About 200 years ago, Luigi Galvani noticed that the legs of a dead frog twitched when he touched them with two metal wires. The two metals were carrying a flow, or **current**, of energy. Galvani had discovered that this energy, **electricity**, makes bodies move. He called this energy 'animal electricity'. However, he did not know where the electricity in a live body comes from.

Other scientists studied the problem. About 80 years ago, scientists found that substances in our bodies, called **chemicals**, create electric signals. These signals send messages along the nerves to the brain. The network of nerves linking up with the brain is called the **nervous system**. Scientists studied the signals which pass along the nervous system. They now know which parts of the brain control the senses.

▶ The first hearing aids were called ear trumpets. People who could not hear well held them to their ears. The ear trumpet made sounds louder and carried the sounds straight into the ear. Hearing aids are much smaller and easier to use now.

7

A network of nerves

The brain is the body's control centre. It receives messages from the senses and sends back orders. The messages move up and down the **spinal cord**. The spinal cord is the 'main road' of the nervous system. It goes down the back bone, through a column of bony rings. The brain and the spinal cord are known as the **central nervous system**. From the spinal cord, 31 smaller nerves branch out in pairs, like minor roads. These nerves divide again and again to form a network of threads to every part of the body. This is called the **peripheral nervous system**.

Nerves do different jobs. The **motor nerves** are responsible for movement. They take instructions from the brain to the **muscles**. Muscles are joined to bones and make the bones move. The **sensory nerves** carry messages about sensations, or feelings like taste or pain, to the brain. There are also some nerves which simply connect other nerves in the brain.

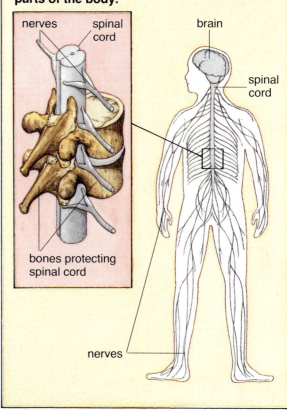

The spinal cord is the main link between the brain and the sensory nerves. Signals from all the sense organs meet in the spinal cord and travel up to the brain. Messages from the brain take the same route back to different parts of the body.

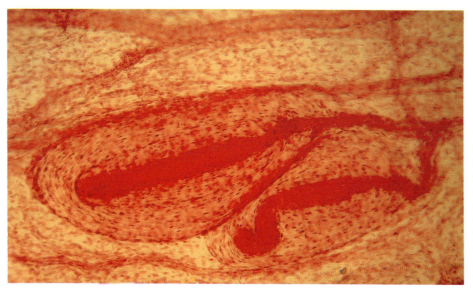

◀ The sensory receptors are very tiny nerve endings in the skin. They pick up signals, such as an itch or touch, from the outside world. This photograph of a receptor has been magnified many times.

A network of nerves

▲ A racing driver runs from his car. His eyes see the flames, his nose smells the smoke, his skin feels the heat. His brain orders his muscles to work fast.

The relay race

How do the sensory nerves work? They work rather like a relay race. Each sensory nerve has a tiny nerve ending called a **sensory receptor**. A receptor picks up a feeling. This changes the chemicals in the receptor and makes an electric current. The electric current travels along the nerves to the brain. The brain takes in the information, sorts it out and tells the motor nerves how to react. It does this by sending an electric signal along the motor nerves.

Suppose you burn your hand. The sensory receptors in your skin pick up the feeling of pain. The receptors in your eyes see the reddened skin. Messages rush to your brain along the nerves. Your brain recognizes what has happened from information it has stored away. It knows that you must move your hand away from what is hurting it. The brain sends messages along the motor nerves to the muscles in your arms. You quickly move your hand away from the heat, before you can even think about it. All this happens very quickly. You do not even realize what is going on in your body.

The bypass

Most messages travel along the sensory nerves to the spinal cord and then to the brain. The brain sends a message back quickly, but it may not be quickly enough. For example, perhaps you pricked your finger with a pin. As soon as your finger touched the pin you took it away again very quickly. The message of pain bypassed the brain. The spinal cord received the message and sent orders straight back to the motor nerves in your arm. You moved your arm without thinking about it. This is called a **reflex action**. All the other actions after the reflex action will pass through the brain.

9

Senses and the brain

Your brain is a soft mass inside your head. It is protected by a 'helmet' of bone. The outer layer of the brain is the **cortex**. It is about a millimetre thick. It is like a piece of cloth folded and crumpled over the rest of the brain. The folds and lumps are made of **grey matter**. This contains a vast number of **cells**. Cells are the tiny parts that make up your body. You have 50 000 million cells in your body. The brain contains about 11 000 million cells. Ten thousand million of these are the nerve cells or **neurons**, in the grey matter. Most nerve cell bodies are in the brain or the spinal cord. Long bunches of threads or nerve fibres spread from these cell bodies to all other parts of the human body. Bundles of white nerve fibres make up the **white matter** in the brain. The white matter is under the layer of grey matter.

The smaller, back part of the brain is called the **cerebellum**. It controls balance and the way your muscles work together. The cerebellum makes your movements smooth, not jerky. The largest part of the brain is called the **cerebrum**. This is the front and upper part, covered by the cortex. The cerebrum is in two parts or **hemispheres**. Most information from your senses goes to the cortex. Nerves from each side of the body cross to the opposite hemisphere of the cerebrum.

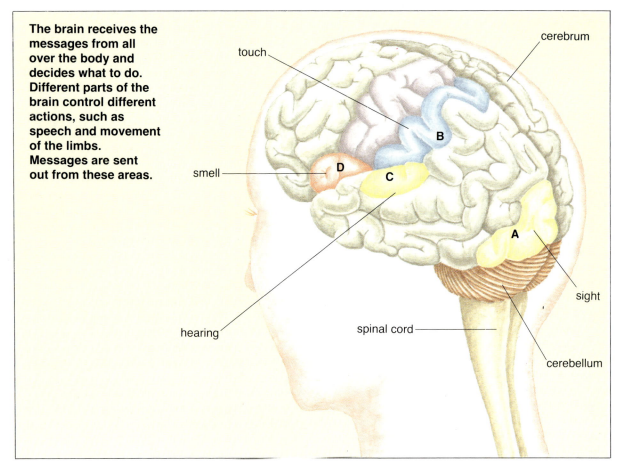

The brain receives the messages from all over the body and decides what to do. Different parts of the brain control different actions, such as speech and movement of the limbs. Messages are sent out from these areas.

Senses and the brain

▲ As this boy looks at the stamps, section A of his brain receives signals from his eyes.

▲ The fingers feel that the cat's fur is soft. This sense of feeling makes it nice to stroke fur, but not something rough like a brick. Section B in the brain deals with touch.

▲ This boy is listening to music on his radio. Section C of the brain deals with hearing.

Control centres

The cortex covering the cerebrum controls all our thoughts, feelings and some of our movements. The work is divided between different centres. The motor centre deals with body movement. This means movements of your face and tongue as well as arms and legs. As a baby learns to speak, motor nerves take messages to the mouth and tongue. These signals tell the baby's muscles how to work to form different words.

Signals from sensory receptors in your skin come to the sensation centre. This centre deals with taste and touch. There are separate parts of the cortex for hearing and sight. The sight centre is right at the back of the brain. The part of the brain where all the thinking is done is right at the front. Nerve cells link all of these parts together.

▲ A girl smells a flower. The sensory cells in her nose send a message to section D in the brain.

Skin and touch

Your sense of touch tells you all about the way things feel. Run your fingers along the surface of this page. You can feel that the paper is smooth. Nerves in your skin send messages to the brain. Skin has an important job to do. The inner layer of skin is called the **dermis**. There are millions of sensory receptors in this inner layer.

Each type of receptor tells the brain about one type of feeling. Some receptors can tell if an object is rough or smooth, soft or hard, dry or wet. Other receptors can feel whether an object is hot or cold. Another set of receptors tell the brain about a hard push, or **pressure**. Put your hand flat on the table. Press the fingers of the other hand over the top of the hand on the table. You can feel how hard one hand is pressing on the other. If you press too hard, it begins to hurt. It something presses on your body or grips you too hard, it could harm you. The pressure receptors tell the brain about this.

The most important feeling is pain. Pain warns the brain that something is harming the body. The pain receptors help you to save your body from injury.

▼ Pain receptors are positioned at different levels of the skin. The receptors nearest to the surface feel the mildest types of pain. Some people cannot feel pain at all. This is a rare problem but it is very dangerous. These people do not know when something is hurting them.

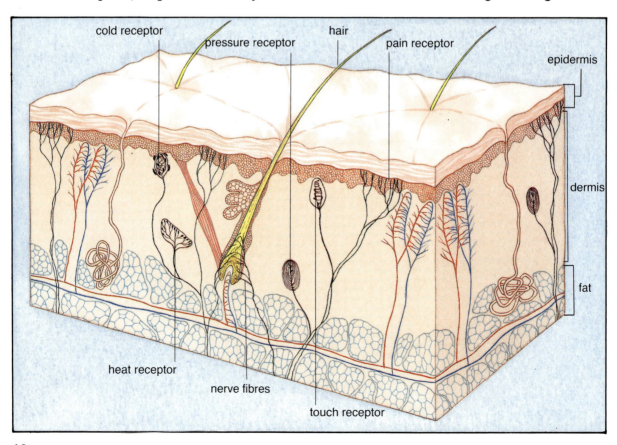

Skin and touch

▼ The tongue is crowded with sensory receptors but not the type that feel heat and cold. You can drink a cup of coffee that would burn your fingers. Because your tongue does not recognize the danger, it is easy to scald the tongue with liquids that are too hot.

Strength of feeling

Some feelings are much sharper than others. If the receptors feel a strong sensation such as heavy pressure, they send an urgent message to the brain. They also send more signals than are sent for a mild feeling. The receptors also send the signals more quickly.

A feeling is also stronger when it comes from one of the places with the most receptors. There are more touch receptors in the tongue, lips, fingertips, and hair roots than in other parts of the body. The nerves are crowded together here, so the brain gets lots of signals. The middle of the back has the fewest receptors. It can be hard to tell just where an itch is.

As it is so important to feel pain, there are pain receptors all over the body. These are located in different parts of the body and pick up different feelings of pain. The mildest form of pain is an itch. If an insect crawls along your arm, some receptors in the outer layer of your skin pick up the tickly feeling of its legs. If the insect stings you, receptors in the next layer feel a sharp pain. Receptors deep in the dermis produce an aching sensation. Pain receptors inside your body tell you if something is wrong inside.

► The hairs on your body have receptors in their roots. They are part of your sense of touch. Cold makes a muscle move so the hair stands up straight. This forms goose pimples on the skin. Our bodies have lots of fine hair. When it stands up straight it traps air and keeps us warm.

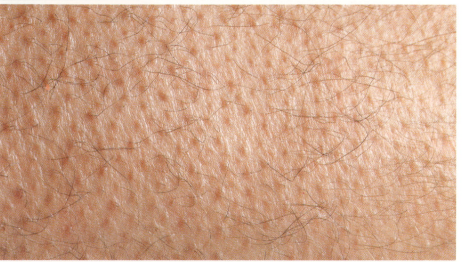

Using touch

Pain is an unpleasant feeling but it helps to keep us safe. Other feelings are very pleasant. If we could not feel them, we would not enjoy so many things in the world. Warm sun on your skin is a pleasant sensation. After the heat, the feeling of a cool shower or the water in a swimming pool is very good, too.

Touch helps you to let other people know how you feel about them. You also use touch to **communicate** your thoughts. If you meet someone, you may shake hands. This is more friendly than just saying 'hello'. If you hug and kiss someone, it shows that you are fond of them. Everyone understands these messages.

People who cannot see rely on touch a great deal. Their fingertips are their 'eyes'. Their sense of touch becomes very sensitive indeed. It helps them to get around. Touch and good hearing tells them about the world they cannot see.

Finding out

People use touch to find out about things. They may need this for their work. A hairdresser can feel if a customer's hair is too dry and needs a special shampoo. The feel of coarse or fine hair tells the hairdresser how best to style it. Carpenters work with wood. It is important for them to know if the surface of the wood is rough or smooth. If it is too rough, the carpenter rubs it with sandpaper until it feels smooth. It is not easy to see the difference. Without a sense of touch, a carpenter would not know what rough or smooth meant.

The human body cannot survive if it gets too cold or too hot. Touch receptors keep things right. If you feel cold, a message goes to your brain. Your brain tells you to move about or put on more clothes to keep warm. If you are ill, you get a fever. You feel hot and this warns you that you are ill.

◀ A sense of touch is very important for communication. This mother gives her son a hug as she reads to him. We can show feelings of love in this way.

Using touch

▲ A tailor uses his sense of touch in choosing cloth and cutting it. Rough cloth might itch the skin but could be used to make a suit. Smooth, soft cloth feels pleasant next to the skin.

▼ The skin helps to control the temperature of the body. If the body gets too hot, pores in the skin open and sweat runs out to help cool the body down.

Inside the body

You have touch receptors inside your body as well as in the skin. In fact, there are receptors in every part of the body, except the brain. Pain receptors tell you if you have a stomachache. They also warn of more serious problems inside your body. Touch receptors tell your brain if your stomach is empty. You feel hungry and want to eat. You can feel hot or cold food and drinks travelling down your throat to your stomach. Waste water is stored in a bag-like part called a **bladder**. If your bladder is full, you can feel the pressure. This tells you to go to the toilet.

Tasting food

You taste food with your tongue. You also use your tongue for talking and eating.

The tongue is covered in small bumps called **papillae**. These give the tongue its rough feel. On each papilla there is a group of cells called **taste buds**. Taste buds are the sensory receptors of taste. An adult has about 9000 taste buds. These are mostly on the tongue but there are also some taste buds on the roof of the mouth and at the back of the throat. A baby has far more taste buds than an adult.

If you look at your tongue through a strong magnifying glass, you can see the taste buds. Each taste bud looks rather like the bud of a flower. Receptor cells are arranged in groups in each taste bud. They form a small hollow. Each receptor cell has tiny taste hairs on the end.

Picking up the taste

The inside of your mouth is always wet. It contains a liquid called **saliva**. When you put food into your mouth, you chew it. Your teeth break the food into small pieces. As you chew, tiny parts of food mix with the saliva. This liquid washes over the taste buds. The tiny hairs on the taste cells pick up the taste of this liquid. The receptor cells then send a message to the nerves in the tongue. These nerves send signals back to the brain.

There are four different types of taste buds. Each type is located on a different part of the tongue and picks up a different taste. The taste buds at the back of the tongue pick up bitter tastes, such as lemon juice. Sour tastes, such as yoghurt, are picked up at the sides. Taste buds at the sides of the front of the tongue pick up salt tastes. The front of the tongue has the taste buds which recognize sweet tastes. There are also cells which can tell if a taste is 'hot' or spicy. They signal the taste of things like curry or pepper to the nerves.

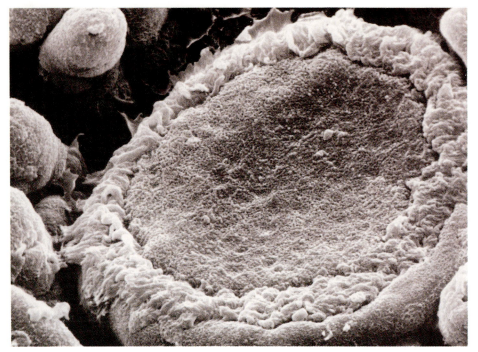

◀ **Look at your tongue in a mirror. You can see the bumps, called papillae, all over the top of your tongue. Each papilla has 100–200 taste buds. They are too small to see in the mirror. This picture of a taste bud has been magnified 1200 times.**

Tasting food

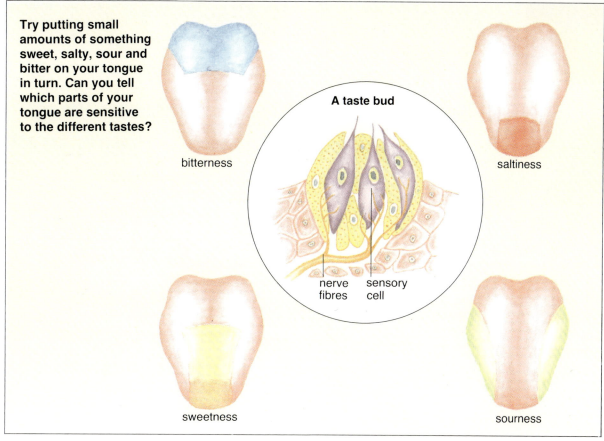

Try putting small amounts of something sweet, salty, sour and bitter on your tongue in turn. Can you tell which parts of your tongue are sensitive to the different tastes?

Why we need taste

A sense of taste can be a life saver. Bitter-tasting plants are often poisonous. Rotten meat could make people ill or even kill them. It tastes nasty. The sense of taste stops people eating bad food.

We need to taste the difference between salt water and fresh water. Salt water would make us sick. Taste also adds to our enjoyment of food. Think how boring eating would be without taste buds.

▶ The front of the tongue picks up the sweet taste of this chocolate ice cream. Taste buds note the flavour of food and whether it is pleasant or unpleasant. Taste signals travel slowly to the brain. It may take you a few seconds to realize what the taste is.

A sense of smell

Behind the nose there is a large space called the **nasal cavity**. When you breathe, you draw air up through your nose. The air passes across the bottom of the nasal cavity. The nose has two jobs, to breathe and to smell. If you want to smell something, you sniff harder than you do when you breathe normally.

The nasal cavity is lined with a sticky substance called **mucus**. At the top of the cavity are the sensory receptors which pick up smells. Tiny sensory hairs extend from the mucus. When you sniff or breathe hard, air is drawn up to the top of the nasal cavity. It passes over the receptors. Certain things, such as flowers, give out tiny bits into the air. These bits are in the air you sniff. The sensory hairs pick up the smell of these bits. The nerves at the ends of the receptor cells send a signal to the brain.

Ten thousand smells

There are more than 10 000 different smells in the world around us. How can your sense of smell sort them all out? You have 15 kinds of sensory receptors in your nasal cavity. These receptors pick up and sort out most of these different smells.

Why do we need a sense of smell? Food which has gone bad smells horrible. The smell warns us not to eat the food. Other smells warn us about dangers.

People and animals all have their own smell. Animals use their sense of smell to find each other, to search for food and to warn them about enemies. Human beings use their eyes to recognize people and things, but new-born babies cannot see very well. Every baby can recognize its mother by her smell.

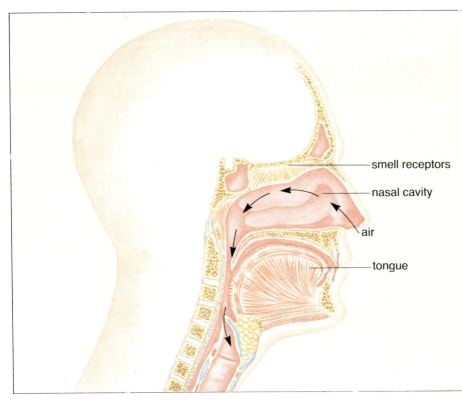

The area of the nasal cavity is only 6 sq cm, but it contains 5 million receptors. These lead to 15 000 nerve fibres which carry information about smell to the brain. Each receptor responds to one type of smell only. The receptors combine to identify the thousands of different smells around us.

A sense of smell

Smell and taste

The picture on the opposite page shows how the mouth, nose and throat are all joined together. There is a strong link between the senses of taste and smell. The sense of taste is not very strong. When you eat something, your sense of smell helps you to get the flavour. When you have a cold, mucus in your nose gets thicker. This extra mucus blocks the sensory hairs and they cannot pick up the smells. This is why you lose some of your sense of taste, because your sense of smell is no longer helping it.

▶ Try this experiment. Ask someone to give you some food while you shut your eyes and hold your nose. Can you tell what you are tasting? It is difficult. We rely on smell to help us taste.

▼ These children know by their sense of smell that their milk is fresh. If milk is left in a warm room, it soon turns sour. The unpleasant smell warns us that it has gone bad.

How we hear

▼ The ear flap funnels sounds down the ear canal to the eardrum. The sound waves strike the eardrum and make it vibrate. The bones in the middle ear pick up the vibrations and pass them to the cochlea. Cells in the cochlea change the vibrations into nerve signals.

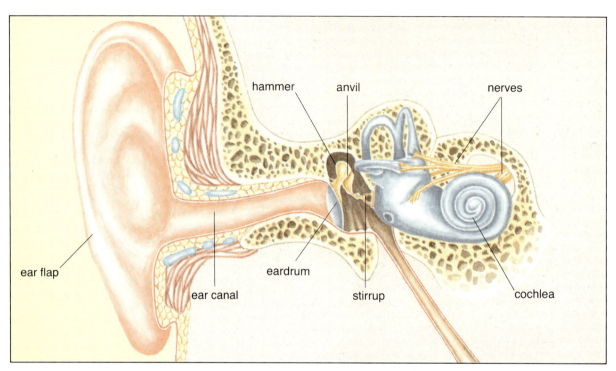

Ears pick up sounds and send hearing messages to the brain. Each ear is divided into three parts. The flaps on the sides of the head are part of the outer ear. A tube leads inside to the middle ear and the inner ear.

Picking up sounds

Sounds travel through the air in waves. The outer ear catches sound waves. The ear flap directs the sounds down a short tube called the ear **canal**. This part of the outer ear is divided from the middle ear by the **eardrum**. The eardrum is like a thin skin across the end of the canal. Sound waves hit the eardrum and make it shake or **vibrate**.

Just behind the eardrum is the middle ear. The middle ear is filled with air. It contains three tiny bones. The names of the bones tell you what they look like. One is the shape of a **hammer**. The next one looks like a blacksmith's **anvil**. The third bone is like the metal part of a saddle where the rider's foot rests. This is the **stirrup** bone. These three tiny bones pick up sound vibrations from the eardrum. The sounds pass to the inner ear.

The inner ear is a very delicate hollow. It is protected by the bones of the head. Inside the hollow there is a tightly coiled tube called the **cochlea**. The cochlea is filled with liquid. Sound vibrations make the liquid move. This motion is picked up by tiny hairs in the cochlea. The hairs are attached to a mass of sensory cells. The sound vibrations are turned into signals which are sent along the nerves to the brain.

How we hear

What can we hear?

Humans cannot hear as many sounds as most animals. Dogs can hear very high-pitched sounds. These sounds make very fast vibrations. Some whistles produce high-pitched sound which dogs can hear but people cannot.

As people get older, their sense of hearing gets weaker. This happens because the hairs in the cochlea start to die. Some older people may become **deaf**. They cannot hear anything at all.

◀ Sometimes we can hear danger before we can see it. Our sense of hearing protects us from harm. Stop, look and listen before you cross a road.

▼ When we talk to each other, we often use our hands to help each other understand what we are trying to say. We also watch each other's faces. Expression can tell us how the other person is feeling.

Ears and balance

▼ The semi-circular canals are shaped like arches. One lies down and the other two stand up. Their arches point away from each other at right angles.

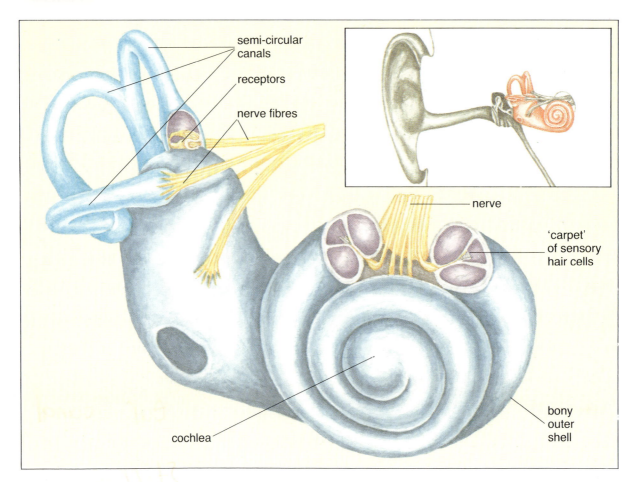

Ears are not just used for hearing. They also help you to keep your balance. Inside the inner ear there are three loops. These are tubes shaped like half circles. They are called **semi-circular canals**. Two of them stand upright and one lies flat. These canals are near the cochlea.

They are filled with the same liquid as the cochlea. The semi-circular canals help us to keep our balance in two ways. They can tell which way the head is moving. They also measure the position of the head. They can tell whether the head is up or down or leaning to one side. How do they do this? The liquid in your inner ear moves as you do. The movements are picked up by tiny hairs in the semi-circular canals. The hairs bend with the movement. If the head turns in one direction, the movement of the liquid makes the hairs bend one way. If the head turns in the opposite direction, the hairs are bent the other way. The hairs are connected to sensory cells. These cells send signals to the brain. The faster the head turns, the more signals the cells produce.

Ears and balance

▲ When we are whirled around on a fairground ride we soon feel giddy. The liquid swirls around inside our ears.

▼ A tightrope walker in a circus has a very highly developed sense of balance. It takes practice to achieve such good balance.

Feeling giddy

When you swing your head round very fast or stand on your head, you feel giddy when you stop. This is because the liquid in the semi-circular canals is still swirling from one side to another. The hairs bend in all directions until the liquid settles. The signals from the cells confuse the brain because the eyes tell the brain you have stopped moving.

An illness of the inner ear can make a person feel giddy all the time. This is called **labyrinthitis**. That part of the inner ear in which the semi-circular canals are found is called the labyrinth.

A view of the world

What happens if you lose your balance? You fall over. You need a sense of balance to keep your body upright and to perform many movements. You could not work or play if you could not keep your balance.

Your sight and pressure receptors help to control your balance by sending the important signals to the brain.

23

Hearing problems

Most parts of the ear are inside the head. The outer bones protect the middle and inner ear. If dust and dirt get inside the ear they can damage it. The ear canal is protected by hairs and by a yellow sticky substance called wax. Any bits of dirt which get into the ear are trapped by the wax so they do not pass into the middle or inner ear.

Even so, we do sometimes get earache or other ear problems. Young children sometimes push small objects into their ears. Sometimes insects fly in and become trapped. Wax may build up and block the ear canal. A doctor can take it out safely. If you have a cold, the extra mucus in your nose stops air getting to your middle ear. This can also give you earache.

▼ At this disco there are flashing lights and deafening music. Very loud noise can damage ears. Some teenagers now have very poor hearing through listening to very loud rock music at discos or concerts.

Hearing problems

◀ A doctor tests how a boy responds to different sounds. The boy wears headphones so that he can only hear the sounds from the machine. He tells the doctor what he can hear. The doctor makes notes.

Illness and deafness

Some ear problems are more serious. There are many reasons why people may have poor hearing, or be completely deaf. Deafness can be caused by illness which affects the hairs in the cochlea or breaks the eardrum. The eardrum may be damaged by a loud noise such as an explosion. If there is a hole in the eardrum the sound waves do not bounce off it properly. A blow to the ear can damage the eardrum.

Sometimes fluid builds up in the middle ear and causes deafness. A doctor can cure this by making a small hole in the eardrum to let the fluid out. The doctor may put a tiny tube called a **grommet** into the eardrum. This keeps the hole open for a while. It stays in the ear for about three months. Many children have grommets in their ears. They cannot feel them. However, they must be very careful not to get water in their ears.

The part of the brain which deals with hearing may be diseased. This also causes deafness because the brain cannot receive the signals from the ears. Some children are born deaf. This may be because the brain is damaged, or because their ears are not properly formed. Some types of deafness can be cured, but others cannot.

Hearing and speech

Hearing and speech work closely together. A child learns to speak by listening to the sounds made by other people. A child who cannot hear, cannot copy those sounds. It is important to check whether young babies have any hearing problems. Doctors can do this by making a different set of sounds, such as very high-pitched ones and very soft ones. The doctors can then see whether the baby reacts to the noise.

Older children and adults are tested for deafness in a different way. They wear headphones and listen to a wide range of sounds made by a machine. Doctors note which sounds the person can hear.

Coping with deafness

▼ Electronic equipment can be used to help children with speech problems. This speech therapist is using a voice-sensitive computer. The picture on the screen shows the girl when she is speaking correctly.

Imagine what it is like to be deaf. You cannot hear people speak. You cannot hear noises that warn you of danger. You cannot listen to the radio or television, or hear pleasant noises like birds singing. Deaf people have to learn to understand sounds in a different way.

Schools for the deaf

Only very deaf people hear nothing at all. Very deaf children go to special schools for the deaf. They are taught to speak and to 'hear' by watching the movements of people's lips. This is called **lip-reading**.

Some deaf people can hear slightly. They know some sounds. Children with a little hearing and children who can lip-read can go to school with children who can hear. However, they may need to sit near the front of the class. Teachers and other children must face a deaf child when they are speaking, so that the deaf child can read their lips. They must make sure that they speak very clearly.

Working with the deaf

Deaf children are taught to understand sounds by feeling vibrations. For example, the teacher can put a balloon between her face and the child's face. The teacher's voice will vibrate against the balloon. The child touches the balloon and feels these vibrations. The deaf child tries to make the same sounds with the same vibrations. With practice, the deaf child can learn to control the voice and to speak.

Coping with deafness

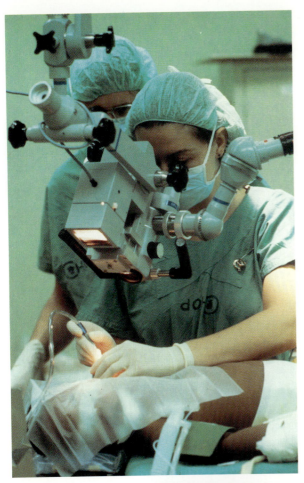

▲ Some hearing problems can be solved by operations. Here, the surgeon looks through a microscope as she operates on a child's ear.

▶ Today hearing aids are very tiny. They fit behind the ear and can hardly be seen. They are powered by small batteries and produce very clear sounds.

Other ways of talking

Lip-reading has been used for many years. The child is taught to recognize how the mouth moves to form different words.

Another way of 'talking' is to use sign language. This helps children who cannot speak or hear. They may learn to make different signs with their hands for every letter of the alphabet. They learn the letters, then how to put them together to form words. It is very slow to talk by spelling out each letter. A quicker sign language uses the hands and body to show whole words or phrases with one sign. Talking in this way is called **signing**.

Special equipment

Some types of deafness can be helped if the person wears a **hearing aid**. This is a tiny machine which fits behind the ear. It makes sounds louder. Sometimes a doctor can perform an **operation** on the inner ear. The doctor puts an **electronic** device inside the ear. This helps the deaf person to hear.

Some television programmes are produced in sign language for deaf people. Others have sentences written out on the screen.

How the eye works

Sight is a very important sense. It tells us a lot about the world around us.

If you look at your eyes in a mirror you can see a coloured part with a black spot in the middle. The coloured part is the **iris**. The black spot is a hole. It is called the **pupil**. Light enters the eye through the pupil. The iris controls the amount of light entering the eye, so that you see a clear picture. The iris is made up of muscle fibres. They lengthen and shorten to make the pupil larger or smaller. If the light is very bright, the pupil becomes smaller so that less light enters the eye. If it is dark, the pupil opens very wide. You do not have to think about it to make your pupil do this. It is called a reflex action.

At the front, the pupil is covered and protected by a layer called the **cornea**. This is like a clear window. You cannot see the cornea when you look in the mirror. Behind the pupil is the **lens**. This is like a small, curved piece of jelly. The lens is held in place by small muscles. The eye works like a camera. Light passes through the lens. It forms an upside-down image at the back of the eye.

Getting the picture

The back of the eye, where the image forms, is called the **retina**. It consists of millions of tiny receptor cells. Each eye has about 6 million special receptors called **cones**. Cones let us see things in bright light. They react to colours. Another type of receptor called **rods** see in dim light. They react to black and white. Each eye has about 120 million rods.

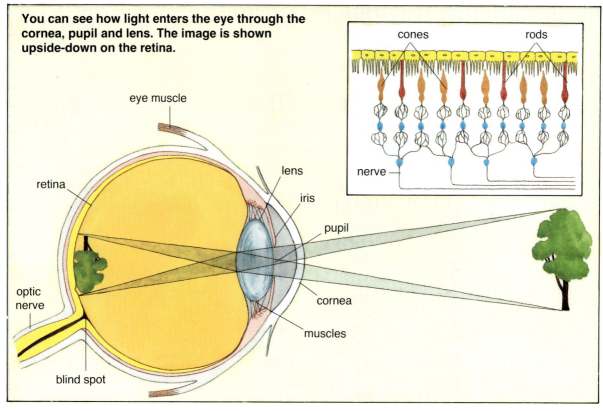

You can see how light enters the eye through the cornea, pupil and lens. The image is shown upside-down on the retina.

How the eye works

The receptor cells send messages to the brain along the nerves. The brain sorts out the information and makes sense of it. It turns the upside-down picture the right way up. It mixes colours and works out how big things are, and how far away they are.

The retina has a **blind spot** where the nerves leave the eye. There are no rods and cones to pick up images on the blind spot. You do not notice this because you have two eyes. Each eye sees a slightly different picture. Your brain puts the two pictures together. You can test this for yourself. Look in front of you. Now cover up one eye. Can you still see the same amount? One eye sees the image that falls on the blind spot of the other eye.

▼ A new-born baby sees the world upside-down. It will be some time before the baby's brain learns to turn the pictures the right way up.

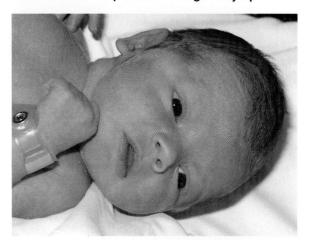

▼ The eye needs protection from dust and dirt which could damage its surface. Your eyelids protect your eyes while you sleep. They also act as windscreen wipers, flicking away dirt. Tears wash the eyes, rather like windscreen washers. The eyelashes help to keep out dust.

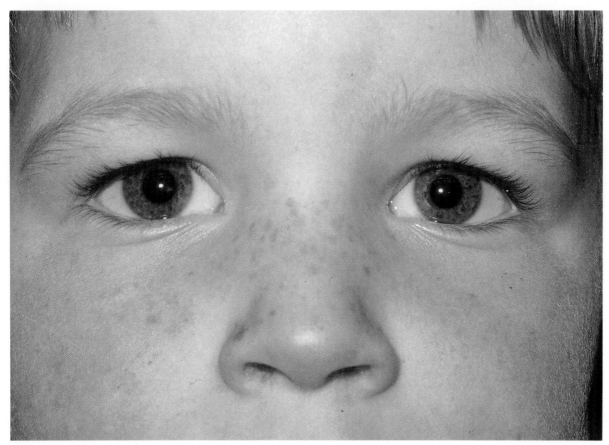

Eye tests

When light enters the eye, the lens bends the light to **focus** it on the retina. The image must fall exactly on the retina, not in front of it or behind it. This does not always happen. Many people have poor sight. They can see, but the lens does not focus the image well. People with poor sight see a blurred picture. Some people are **short-sighted**. Short-sighted people cannot see distant objects clearly. Their eyeballs are long in shape, so the lens focuses the light in front of the retina. Short-sight can be corrected with lenses made of plastic or glass. The lenses curve in like a bowl. They are **concave** lenses. This type of lens spreads out the light before it reaches the pupil. Then the lens of the eye can focus this light on the retina. Some people have **long-sight**. Long-sighted people can see distant objects but close objects look blurred. The lens of the eye focuses the light behind the retina. This is corrected with lenses which curve outwards. They are **convex**. These lenses cause the light rays to bend before they reach the pupil. Then, the lens of the eye can focus the light on the retina. Long-sighted people often have eyeballs that are shorter than usual. Many people become long-sighted as they grow older. This happens because the muscles around the eye weaken. The muscles that control the lens become too weak to help the lens change shape. The lens can no longer bend the light so that it focuses where it should.

Different colours

The cones on the retina sort out the colours you see. Some people have faulty cones. They cannot tell the difference between certain colours, particularly red and green. These people are **colour blind**. Colour blindness affects more men than women.

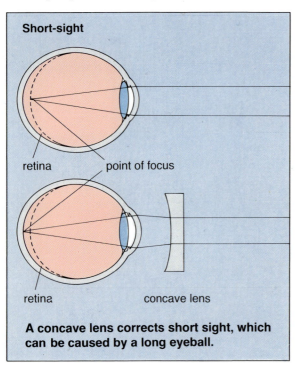

A concave lens corrects short sight, which can be caused by a long eyeball.

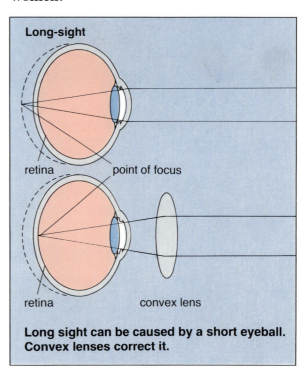

Long sight can be caused by a short eyeball. Convex lenses correct it.

Eye tests

▼ Look at this picture. It is a test for colour blindness. Can you see the number hidden among the dots? If you are colour blind, you cannot see the number because you cannot distinguish between the different colours.

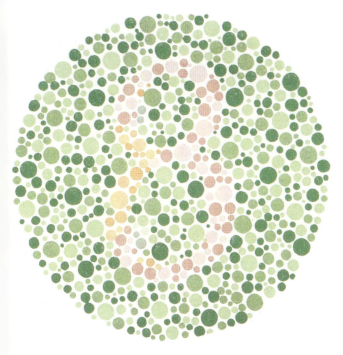

The eye test

If you cannot see clearly, you can have your eyes tested by an **optometrist**. The optometrist shows you charts with letters and patterns on them. You say what you can see. There are special cards to test for colour blindness. These have patterns and numbers in different coloured dots. Colour-blind people can only see dots on the cards. They cannot see any difference in the colours.

If you find it difficult to see any of the letters or patterns, the optometrist will know that you need spectacles. He or she will have to find out what kind of lenses to put in. The optometrist puts some frames in front of your eyes and tries different lenses in them. You say which ones help you to see best.

The spectacles are made by an **optician**. You can choose the frames you like best. Opticians can also make **contact lenses**. These are tiny discs of plastic which fit straight onto the eyeball. Some people prefer to wear contact lenses.

► Sometimes poor sight can develop without you realising it. You should have your eyes tested regularly to make sure that they are all right. If you find it difficult to see any of the letters, you may need spectacles for some things such as reading.

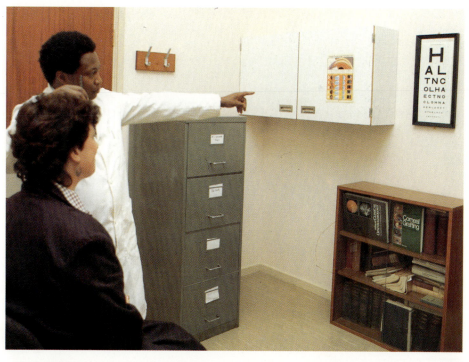

Problems with the eyes

Doctors can tell a lot about your health by looking at your eyes. If you are fit and healthy, the white part looks clear. The proper name for the whites of the eye is the **sclera**. Sometimes you can see tiny red threads running through the sclera. This is a sign of tiredness or poor health. Eyes that look red like this are called bloodshot.

Some illnesses make the sclera look yellow. This is because the blood is carrying a yellow substance. Yellow eyes may be the first sign of the illness called **jaundice**. The eyes can tell us in this way when something is wrong inside the body.

Eye infections

The eye is delicate. A thin, clear skin covers the front of the eye to protect it. It also lines the eyelids. Dust or disease can affect this part of the eye and make it red and sore. Sometimes the eye feels sticky and it is difficult to open it after sleep. This problem is called **conjunctivitis**. It often affects both eyes at once. Doctors can treat conjunctivitis with eye drops or an ointment. Hay fever and colds also make the eyes sore. They water a lot and feel uncomfortable.

Some eye diseases are more serious. The lens of the eye may become cloudy. This is called **cataract**. Sometimes too much fluid builds up in the eye and causes pressure. This disease of the eye is **glaucoma**. It is very painful. Glaucoma can damage the retina and the nerves. Cataracts and glaucoma can both lead to blindness, if they are not treated. It is important to go to a doctor as soon as an eye problem begins. If an eye infection is not treated quickly, it may harm the eye forever. Also an infection can easily be passed from one person to another.

▼ Illness can affect the appearance of the eye. This person is suffering from conjunctivitis and the whites of the eye, called the sclera, are bloodshot.

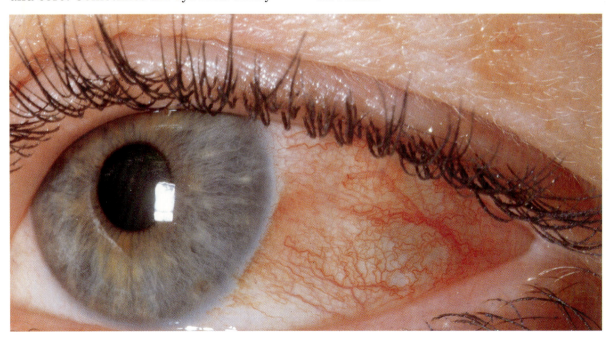

Problems with the eyes

▲ Straw, dust and pollen can cause hay fever. This makes the eyes water because little bits in the air get into the lining of the eyelid. The eyes become red and itchy.

▶ The fumes of onions can make us cry. The eyes need frequent washing with tears and wiping by the lids. Fumes in the air, pain, soreness or something in your eye may produce extra tears. They overflow and you weep.

Damage to the eye

It is easy to scratch the eyeball. This can leave a scar or damage the eyesight. If you get some dust or an insect in your eye, it feels very painful. The eye begins to water. It is trying to wash away the object. You must be very careful when you try to get anything out of your eye. Something sharp could cut the cornea and damage your eye. It is often best to ask a skilled person, like a nurse or doctor for help.

Treating eyes

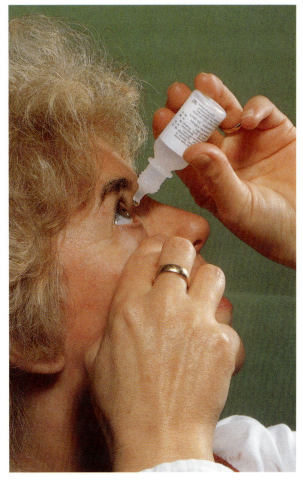

▼ Eye drops are quite easy to use. The patient blinks and spreads the drops through the eye.

Any doctor or nurse can treat a common eye infection, such as conjunctivitis. More serious problems and rare diseases have to be treated in hospital. Many hospitals have a clinic just for the treatment of eye problems. A large town may have a separate eye hospital.

A visit to the doctor

The study and treatment of the eye and eye diseases is called **ophthalmic** medicine. This includes all problems with sight, eye diseases and damage from accidents.

A doctor cannot always tell what is wrong just by looking at the outside of the eyes. He or she uses a tool with a magnifying lens that makes things look bigger. It is called an **ophthalmoscope**. An ophthalmoscope also has a small light bulb inside it. The mirror reflects the light from the bulb, so that the doctor can see into the eye. The doctor puts one end in front of the patient's eye and looks through the pupil to the retina.

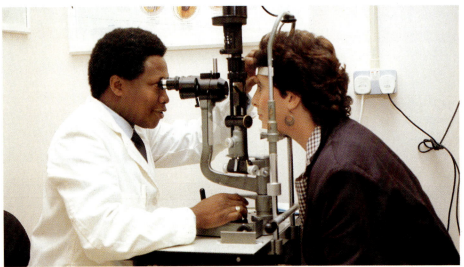

◀ This doctor is examining a patient's eyes. The patient's face is supported by a chin rest. The doctor looks through a magnifying lens. A narrow beam of light shows up details of different parts of the eye, such as the iris or the lens.

Eye operations

Some eye problems can only be put right by surgery. Eye surgery is very hard to do. The eye is very small. It is easy to damage it. Ophthalmic surgeons have to be very skilful.

Sometimes children have a weak eye muscle. This may make one eye pull to the side. This is called a **squint**. Very bad squints are treated by an operation to tighten the muscle.

One type of cataract makes the lens of the eye go hard. Then the lens cannot change shape to focus. Surgeons can remove the diseased lens and replace it with a new, plastic one. Putting another piece into the body like this is called an **implant**.

Sometimes an illness turns the cornea of the eye milky white. A surgeon can remove part of the diseased cornea and add on a healthy cornea. This is called a **graft**.

If the retina is torn in an accident, fluid seeps through the hole and lifts the retina up. This is called a detached retina. It can be fixed in place again by an operation.

Glaucoma can sometimes be treated with special eye drops. If this fails, the patient usually needs an operation to drain the fluid.

▼ This is a photograph of the inside of the eye taken through the pupil. The darker patch in the centre of the retina is a concave area which reflects the light around the retina. Surgeons can use pictures like this to see what is wrong with an eye.

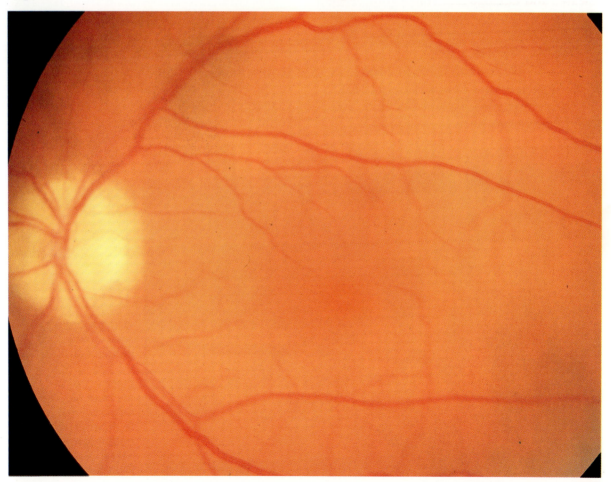

Blindness

Shut your eyes and stand up. Could you walk to the other side of the room? It is quite frightening when you cannot see where you are going. You grope around with your hands and bump into things. Imagine what it would be like to be like this all the time.

Some people are born completely blind. They have never seen any of the things in the world around them. Others become blind through illness or an accident.

Some people are partially blind. They can make out shapes but they cannot read a book or tell colours apart.

Schools for the blind

Blind people have to learn to cope without their sight. Teachers help them to use their other senses instead of their eyes. Blind people can learn to do almost anything. They can work in offices using typewriters and computers. They can be trained for other jobs using special machines. Blind children may go to a special school. They learn the usual school subjects as well as how to look after themselves.

Getting around

The first thing blind and partially blind people have to learn is how to get around safely. There are dangers inside and outside the home. Some blind people have a guide dog. These dogs are trained to lead their owners along. The dogs are even trained to look up as well, so their owners do not bang their heads. A guide dog wears a special, firm harness. The blind person holds the other end of the harness. The dog is trained to recognize traffic. It waits until it is safe to cross the road.

Many blind people use canes to feel their way about. They tap the ground in front of them. This tells them if there is anything in the way. A white cane tells other people that the person is blind. They can help the blind person cross the road.

◀ Crossing a busy road can be very dangerous for a blind person. In some places, traffic lights at crossings make a noise when it is safe to cross. Many blind people use a guide dog to help them find their way.

Blindness

► This children's book has been made using braille. Blind people can read and write using the braille alphabet. They feel the pattern of dots with their fingers and write with a special typewriter.

▼ Blind people can often learn to do complicated jobs by using specially adapted machinery. This man is using a machine to help him study.

The sense of touch

Blind people learn to use their senses of touch, hearing and smell to replace their sight. These senses often become sharper. Blind people can learn to read **braille**. This is a special alphabet of raised dots. Blind people feel the dots with their fingers. A Frenchman, called Louis Braille, thought of this alphabet. He lost his sight because of an accident when he was three years old.

Equipment for the blind

Blind people can listen to 'talking' books. Someone reads the book into a tape recorder. Blind people can borrow the tapes from a library.

Knobs on things in the home, like cookers, can be changed for blind people to use. They feel bumps on the special knobs so they know which one to use. They can buy a device to put in a cup when they pour a hot drink. The device makes a noise so that the blind person knows when the cup is full.

Lost to the world

Have you ever been on a train when it goes into a tunnel? If this happens when there are no lights on in the train, suddenly everything is black. The air in the tunnel can make your ears block up. You cannot see or hear properly. This sudden cut-off of signals to your brain can be frightening. In a cinema or in a theatre, the lights are turned down slowly. People might panic if they were suddenly in complete darkness.

A loss of any of the senses like this is called **sensory deprivation**. A long time without signals from the sense organs makes people feel very strange. They may forget who they are. The brain is confused when there are no signals from the outside world. People have suffered from sensory deprivation in prisons or trapped underground after an accident. People who have been rescued from sensory deprivation say they felt fear and sadness for a long time afterwards.

▼ **The blindfolded child has lost all sense of direction playing Blindman's Buff. This is fun for a short time as a party game. We cannot put up with sensory deprivation for too long however. It can become frightening.**

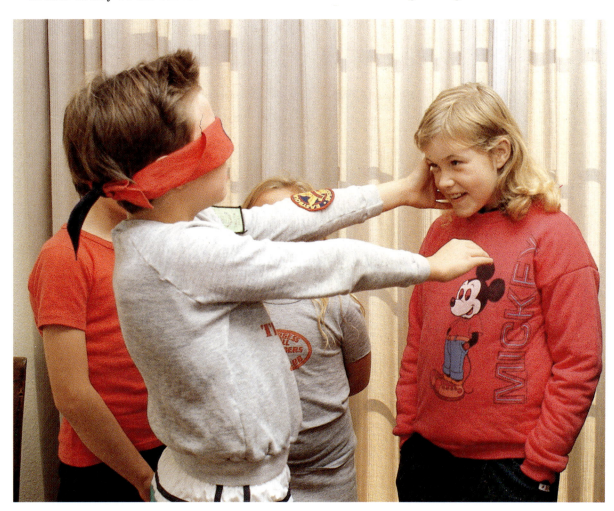

Lost to the world

Mysteries and marvels

Some people have learned to control their minds so they do not notice their senses. No one knows how this works. Many people in India and other parts of the world practise deep and peaceful thought. They sit quietly with closed eyes and seem to be asleep. They seem to close off the parts of their brains that hear, or feel a touch.

Some people can even stop parts of their body working normally. They are able to slow their heart down so that it is barely beating. They do not seem to notice cold or heat. It takes years of practice to have such control over your mind.

Holy men called **fakirs** have learned how to control their bodies so they do not feel pain. They can walk or lie on broken glass, hot coals or a bed of nails without feeling pain.

▲ A tea-tasting session. Expert tea-tasters can tell the difference between many teas from all over the world. They use their sense of smell as well as taste. They practice and concentrate to develop these senses.

► How is it done? This Bulgarian has learned how to walk across burning coals. He does not seem to feel any pain. Never try this yourself!

Safety first

We need our senses. They do important work. They help to protect our bodies. They tell the brain what is going on. It is easy to harm our senses. They are vital to us, so we have to make sure we protect them.

Wear a helmet

We cannot live without a brain to control our body. The bones in the head protect the brain but that is not always enough. A coal miner or a worker on a building site could be hit on the head. In many jobs people must wear helmets for safety. Helmets also give extra protection in dangerous pastimes such as motor cycling.

Sensitive skin

Hot sun can burn the skin. The skin must be protected from burns, scalds or harm from chemicals and other materials, too. People who work in great heat or with dangerous chemicals should wear special clothes and gloves. Clothing treated with a heat-resistant finish does not catch fire.

Protecting the nose and throat

If we breathe in dust or fumes, they can damage the nose, throat and lungs. There are dangers in everyday life. People who live in busy towns breathe in exhaust fumes from the traffic. Cigarettes affect the sense of taste and smell and damage the lungs. Some chemicals have dangerous fumes. People who work with chemicals or in dusty conditions need to wear masks over their noses. The masks stop bits of dust or fumes in the air passing into the nose.

◀ Many workers need special clothing to protect themselves. This worker is sandblasting metal. His skin is covered by overalls and gloves. His eyes and ears are protected by a helmet.

Safety first

▲ Aircraft noise can damage the hearing of people who live near an airport. Decibel levels must be measured regularly for safety.

▼ Bright light and dazzling snow can blind people. These mountaineers are wearing dark goggles to cut out the glare. They are at the summit of Rani Peak in the Himalayas.

Damage to the ears

Very loud noise can damage your hearing. Noise levels are measured in **decibels**. Normal conversation is about 60 decibels. The level of a rock concert may be over 100 decibels. Some machinery is 110 decibels, and a road drill 120 decibels. A jet aircraft has a noise level of 130 decibels. These levels are dangerous. People who are near these noises for a long time need to wear ear plugs or special earmuffs. They block out some of the noise.

Look after your eyes

Sharp objects can pierce your eyes and blind you. Always be careful when using scissors, knives and any pointed objects. Never put them near anyone's eyes.

At work, people may be at risk from splashing chemicals, splinters, sparks from machinery, and dust. They may have to wear protective spectacles or goggles. Dark glasses and eyeshields protect the eyes from dazzling light. Working in bad light or watching words on a screen or **VDU** all day long can cause eye strain. The first signs of eye strain are tiredness and headaches.

To the rescue

▼ Household chemicals which burn the skin include bleach, caustic soda, and paint stripper. If any of these are spilled on the skin wash the affected area in cold water for at least 10 minutes, under a running tap if possible. Remove any contaminated clothing.

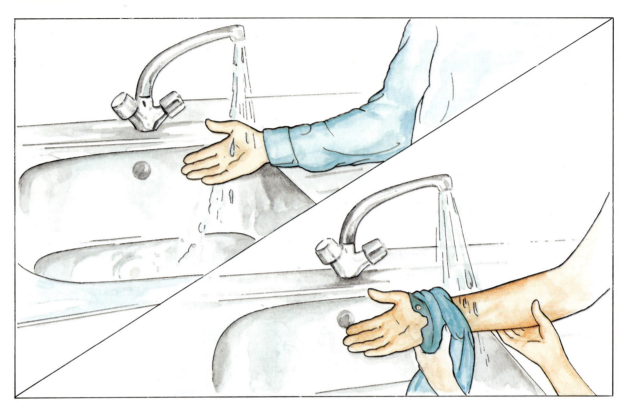

What do you do if someone has an accident and needs help? Many classes teach a simple form of medical treatment called first aid. Anyone can learn how to give first aid. First aid can help save a person's life.

If you do not know about first aid and there is an emergency, the main thing is to stay calm. Call an adult or telephone for an ambulance.

Damage to the skin

Damage to the skin can be burns, cuts or grazes. Burns should be cooled off by applying something cold for at least ten minutes, or until the cold lessens the heat of the burn. Replace the cold object when it gets warm. Cover the burn with a clean, dry bandage. Do not use cotton wool. Never use creams on a burn. Deep burns may hurt less than small burns. This is because the nerve ends in the skin are damaged.

Many chemicals can burn the skin. Wash the chemical off the skin with plenty of cold water. Remove any clothes which have the chemical on them. Anybody who has been burnt should see a doctor.

Cuts and grazes should be washed in cold water. Dirt or grit should be carefully washed away from the wound. Use an **antiseptic**. It kills germs and keeps them from getting into the body. Carefully put a dressing on the cut to stop the bleeding and to keep it clean.

To the rescue

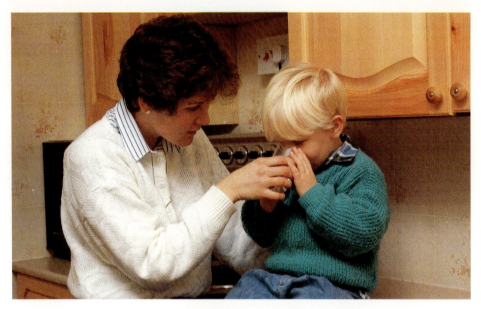

◀ Small sips of cold water help a scalded mouth or throat. Comfort the patient at the same time.

Never stick anything in your ear. Some things may float out with water. Do not try to dig anything out. If an object or insect does not come out easily, see a doctor.

Damage to the mouth

The soft linings of the mouth, throat and tongue are easily scalded. If someone swallows hot liquid the linings swell and hurt. Try to give the person cold water or milk to sip. Loosen any tight clothing around the neck, such as a collar or a scarf, so that the person can breathe better. Get the injured person to hospital.

Ears, nose and eyes

An insect in the ear can sometimes be washed out with lukewarm water. Grit or an insect in the eye may be quite easy to remove. Pull down the lower lid. Remove the object by wiping toward the inner corner of the eye with a clean cloth or tissue. Do not keep rubbing the area. If the object does not come out easily see a doctor.

If you have a nosebleed, sit with a bowl under your nose, or lean over a basin. Press the sides of your nose together for ten minutes. Breathe through your mouth and spit any blood into the bowl. If the bleeding does not stop, carry on pressing your nose for another ten minutes. If the bleeding still does not stop you should see a doctor.

Did you know?

★ A sensory nerve can send out 1000 signals a second.

★ When speed is not important, nerve signals travel at 50 centimetres a second. When speed is important, such as when we feel pain, the signals can travel at 100 metres a second!

★ Are we getting brainier? In 1860, the average weight of a man's brain was 1372 grams. Now it is 1432 grams.

★ Before a baby is born, nerve cells form in the baby's brain at the rate of 250 000 a minute. Very few are formed after birth.

★ After the age of twenty, 10 000 nerve cells in the brain die each day and are not replaced.

★ The world's smelliest substance is a chemical called ethyl mercapatan. It smells like a mixture of rotting cabbage, garlic, onions and sewer gas.

★ Most children can hear sounds which measure between 10 and 140 decibels. Most adults can hear sounds which measure as low as 0 decibels.

★ Sounds of 120 or 130 decibels are painful to the ears. Sounds above 150 decibels will cause deafness. Sounds above 175 decibels will kill a person.

★ The pitch of a sound, whether it is high or low, is measured in cycles per second. The speaking voice ranges between 100 and 150 cycles per second. We can hear sounds between a low rumble of 10 cycles per second up to a high pitched hiss of 20 000 cycles per second. Between these two, we can hear more than 1500 different pitches of sound. Women can hear sounds at higher pitches than men can.

★ Porpoises, bats and moths can hear very high-pitched sounds of 100 000 cycles per second. Dogs can hear sounds which are nearly as high.

★ There are only three 'primary' colours. These are red, blue and yellow. We can recognize 10 000 000 shades of colour, all based on these three primary colours.

▼ Dolphins have the best sense of hearing of any animals. It is nearly twice as good as bats, who are next on the list, and 14 times better than humans.

Did you know?

★ We blink every 2–10 seconds, for 0.3 seconds.

★ The Czechs suffer more from red/green colour-blindness than any other people.

★ The brain is one-fiftieth of the total body weight, yet it uses one-fifth of the body's energy.

★ You can see better in the dark or in dim light if you look slightly to one side of an object. This is because the rods, which work in dim light, are at the sides of the retina.

★ Your sense of smell and taste fades as you grow older. It begins to fade as soon as you are born. By the age of 20 you have 82 per cent left. By the time you are 60 only 38 per cent is left and by 80 only 28 per cent is left.

▶ Many things have been invented to help people who have faulty senses. This robotic dog was invented in Japan to act as a guide dog for the blind. It has electronic 'eyes' which can 'see' objects in its way.

▼ This is a greatly magnified section of the auditory nerve. It carries messages from the 25 000 receptors in the ear, to the brain.

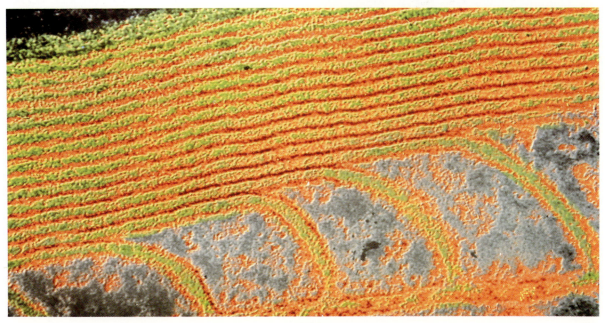

Glossary

antiseptic: a liquid or lotion which kills germs
anvil: a tiny bone in the middle ear
bladder: a hollow organ which holds the body's waste water
blind spot: a point where the nerve leaves the back of the eye. This point does not pick up light. If part of an image falls on your blind spot, you cannot see it with that eye
braille: a special alphabet for blind people. It is made up of patterns of raised dots. Each pattern stands for a letter of the alphabet. A blind person feels the patterns with the fingertips
brain: the 'computer' in our heads, which controls everything we do
canal: a narrow channel
cataract: a change in the lens of the eye which makes it cloud over so that what you see is blurred. This can happen slowly over about 30 years. Sometimes the lens becomes hard. This can make someone short-sighted or even blind
cells: the 'building blocks' of our bodies. They are very tiny. Every living thing is made up of cells
central nervous system: the brain and the spinal cord which form the main part of the nervous system
cerebellum: an area at the base of the brain. It controls balance and helps with movement
cerebrum: the largest part of the brain. It is responsible for thought, intelligence, memory and feelings, and plays a part in directing our movements
chemical: any substance which can change when joined or mixed with another substance
cochlea: a coiled tube in the inner ear in which sound vibrations are turned into nerve signals
colour blind: when someone cannot make out the difference between colours, usually red and green
communicate: to exchange information
concave: curved inwards
cones: cells at the back of the eye. They see colours and work in bright light
conjunctivitis: an eye infection. The inside of the eyelid becomes inflamed and the rims of the eye look red and feel sticky
contact lens: a small lens which fits on to the front of the eyeball
convex: curving outwards
cornea: the clear outer covering of the eyeball
cortex: the wrinkled outer layer of the brain
current: a flow or stream of water, air or electricity
deaf: unable to hear some sounds or anything at all
decibel: a unit for measuring noise levels
dermis: the inner layer of the skin
eardrum: the thin skin between the end of the ear canal and the middle ear. Vibrations made by sounds on the eardrum are passed to the bones in the middle ear
electricity: a type of power
electronic: describes machines controlled by electricity or containing special electrical apparatus
fakir: a holy man of the Moslem or Hindu religions
focus: the point at which light rays meet to make a clear image
glaucoma: a disease of the eye in which fluid builds up inside the eye. The pressure stops blood reaching the nerves at the back of the eye and this kills them
graft: to replace a diseased or injured part of the body, such as skin, bone, or part of the eye, with a healthy living part from another part of the patient's body or from someone else's
grey matter: the jelly-like substance which makes up the outer layer of the brain
grommet: tiny tube made from plastic material which is fitted into the ear
hammer: a tiny bone in the middle ear
hearing aid: a small device which helps people to hear better. It is powered by a small battery and makes sounds louder in the ear
hemisphere: half of a sphere or ball
implant: a new part of the body, which is put in after a diseased part has been removed
iris: the coloured part of the eyeball. It contains muscles which allow more or less light in
jaundice: a disease of the liver, the organ in the body which cleans the blood. Jaundice means 'being yellow'. The illness makes the skin and the eyeballs look yellow
labyrinthitis: inflammation of the labyrinth. The labyrinth is another name for the inner ear
lens: the transparent, jelly-like window through which light enters the eye
lip-reading: understanding what a person is saying by watching the movement of his or her lips
long-sight: being able to see distant things clearly, but close things look blurred
motor nerves: the nerves which control movement by taking orders from the brain to the muscles

Glossary

mucus: a sticky substance produced by some parts of the body such as the inside of the nose or stomach. Infections such as a cold cause too much mucus to be produced in the nose

muscles: bundles of fibres which tighten and relax to move our bones

nasal cavity: the hollow area in the upper part of the nose. It contains the sense cells of smell

nerves: cells and fibres like tiny threads which carry messages between the brain and the rest of the body

nervous system: the system of nerves which runs from the brain right through the body. It controls all our movements and feelings

neuron: a nerve cell

operation: opening the body to repair a part inside

ophthalmic: to do with the eye

ophthalmoscope: an instrument for viewing inside the eye. It is fitted with a lens

optician: someone who makes spectacles and contact lenses

optometrist: someone who tests a person's sight

papilla: one of the bumps on the tongue. The papillae include groups of cells that sense taste

peripheral nervous system: the nerves which branch out from the brain and spinal cord to every part of the body

pressure: the amount of force of one body or thing against another

pupil: the black hole in the centre of the eye

reflex action: an instant reaction such as dropping something hot. Messages are sent to and from the spinal cord along the nerves. The messages bypass the brain, for speed

retina: a layer at the back of the eye, sensitive to light

rods: cells at the back of the eye. They can see in dim light but can only make out black and white

saliva: the liquid produced in the mouth to help break down food and wash it down the throat

sclera: the white part of the eye around the iris

semi-circular canal: one of the three tubes in the inner ear which control balance

sense: parts all over the body which take in information about the outside world and pass messages to the brain. The five senses are sight, hearing, smell, touch and taste

sensory deprivation: the sudden cutting-off of one or all of the senses

sensory nerve: a nerve which takes messages from the senses to the brain

sensory receptor: the nerve cells at the end of the sensory nerves. They receive the signals and pass them along the nervous system to the brain

short-sight: only able to see things close by. Anything further away is blurred

signing: 'talking' by using a sign language for deaf people. Each letter of the alphabet is shown by a different sign with the hands

spectacles: a pair of frames with lenses in them for correcting poor sight

spinal cord: the central nerve which runs from the brain through the column of bones down the middle of the back

squint: when the eyes are looking in different directions, often making somebody cross-eyed

stirrup: a tiny bone in the middle ear

taste buds: the organs of taste, which are found mainly on the tongue

VDU: visual display unit. The screen of a computer

vibrate: to move very quickly to and fro or to shake

white matter: the mass of nerve fibres which make up the central part of the brain and spinal cord

Index

animal electricity 7
animals 5, 18, 20, 44
anvil bone 20

balance 10, 22, 23
birds 5
blindness 6, 36, 37
blind spot 29
Braille, Louis 37
braille 37
brain 4, 6, 7, 8, 9, 10, 11, 12, 13, 14, 15, 16, 18, 20, 22, 23, 25, 29, 38, 39, 40, 44, 45
burns 9, 40, 42

cataract 32, 35
cells 10, 11, 16, 20, 22, 23, 29, 44
central nervous system 8
cerebellum 10
cerebrum 10, 11
chemical 7, 9, 40, 41, 44
chemical burns 42
cochlea 20, 21, 22, 25
colds 32
colour blindness 30, 31
cones 29, 30
conjunctivitis 32, 34
contact lenses 31
cornea 28, 33, 35
cortex 10, 11
cuts 42

deafness 6, 21, 25, 26, 27, 44
dermis 12, 13
detached retina 35

earache 24
ear canal 20, 24
eardrum 20, 25
ears 6, 20, 22, 24, 25, 38, 43
ear trumpet 6
electricity 7, 9
eyes 4, 5, 6, 9, 18, 23, 28, 29, 30, 32, 33, 34, 35, 36, 37, 39, 41, 45
eye tests 31

fakir 39
feeling 11, 12, 13, 14, 15
first aid 42, 43

Galvani, Luigi 7
giddiness 23
glaucoma 32, 35
grafts 35
grazes 42
grey matter 10

hammer bone 20
hay fever 32
hearing 4, 6, 11, 14, 20, 21, 22, 24, 25, 26, 37, 39, 41, 44
hearing aid 27
Hippocrates 6

implants 35
inner ear 20, 22, 23, 24
insects 5
iris 28

labyrinthitis 23
lens 28, 30, 31, 35
lip-reading 26, 27
long-sight 30

medicine 6
middle ear 20, 24, 25
motor nerves 8, 9, 11
mouth 11, 16, 19, 26, 43
movement 7, 8, 10, 11, 22, 23
mucus 18, 19, 24
muscles 8, 9, 10, 11, 28, 30, 35

nasal cavity 18
nerve fibres 10
nerves 4, 7, 8, 9, 10, 12, 13, 16, 18, 20, 29
nervous system 7
neurons 10
noise levels 41
nose 6, 18, 19, 24, 40, 43
nosebleeds 43

ophthalmic medicine 34, 35
ophthalmoscope 34
optometrist 31
outer ear 20

pain 5, 8, 9, 12, 13, 14, 15, 39, 44
papillae 16
peripheral nervous system 8
pressure 12, 13, 15, 23, 32
pupil 28, 30, 34

reflex action 9, 28
retina 29, 30, 32, 34, 45
rods 29, 45

saliva 16
scalding 40, 43
sclera 32
semi-circular canals 22, 23
sensory deprivation 38
sensory nerves 8, 9, 44
sensory receptors 9, 11, 12, 13, 16, 18
short-sight 30
sight 4, 5, 6, 11, 23, 28, 30, 31, 36
sign language 27
skin 9, 11, 12, 13, 15, 40, 42
smell 4, 5, 6, 18, 19, 37, 44, 45
sounds 20, 21, 25, 26, 44
spectacles 6, 31
speech 11, 25, 26
spinal cord 8, 9, 10
squint 35
stirrup bone 20

taste 4, 8, 11, 16, 17, 19, 45
taste buds 16, 17
thought 11, 14
throat 16, 19, 40, 43
tongue 11, 13, 16, 43
touch 4, 5, 11, 12, 13, 14, 15, 37, 39

wax 24
white matter 10